LEGACY

The Fundamental Principals of
Family & Financial Planning

LEGACY

The Fundamental Principals of Family & Financial Planning

ALLEN GORE, MD, MBA

LEGACY
Published by Purposely Created Publishing Group™

Copyright © 2018 Allen Gore

All rights reserved.

No part of this book may be reproduced, distributed or transmitted in any form by any means, graphic, electronic, or mechanical, including photocopy, recording, taping, or by any information storage or retrieval system, without permission in writing from the publisher, except in the case of reprints in the context of reviews, quotes, or references.

Printed in the United States of America

ISBN: 978-1-948400-72-5

Special discounts are available on bulk quantity purchases by book clubs, associations and special interest groups. For details email: sales@publishyourgift.com or call (888) 949-6228.

For information logon to: www.PublishYourGift.com

*I dedicate this book to my mentors,
my children, my beautiful wife,
and God.*

Table of Contents

Introduction:
Why Money and Family 1

Chapter 1:
Don't Spend What You Don't Have 9

Chapter 2:
Steady Cash Flow 17

Chapter 3:
Cash, Not Credit 23

Chapter 4:
Turn Up Your Value 31

Chapter 5:
Get Mentors 37

Chapter 6:
Avoid the Extra Pennies 43

Chapter 7:
Own Money..49

Chapter 8:
A Membership Goes a Long Way......................57

Chapter 9:
Insure Yourself and Your Things 63

About the Author 71

Introduction

Why Money and Family?

A large number of people unfortunately still appear to believe that you can't buy happiness.

Maybe you can't, but you can buy comfort, you can save enough to have security, and you can give yourself more options and a richer life in more ways than one. If you understand the value of money, not only will you open doors for yourself, but you'll be able to recognize when others are trying to shut them on you. Knowledge is power, but application is key.

Four concepts you must understand to get the most from this book:

- Your money does not control you, you control your money.

- Rome wasn't built in a day. It takes work to build an empire.

- You have to prioritize yourself before you help someone else.

- Money isn't everything, but you can't buy anything without it.

Terms that you need to remember:

- LLC: limited liability company
- APR: annual percentage rate
- Assets: property owned by a person or company regarded as having value
- Cash Flow: the total amount of money being transferred in an out of a person or business
- Interest (Simple/Compound): based on the principal amount/principal & accumulated interest
- Percentage: the proportion or share in relation to a whole
- 401K: retirement savings plan sponsored by an employer

NOTES:

Date:_____

NOTES:

_____

_____

_____

_____

_____

_____

_____

_____

_____

_____

_____

_____

_____

_____

_____

Date:_____

NOTES:

Date:_____

"An investment in knowledge always pays the best interest."

—Benjamin Franklin

Chapter 1

Don't Spend What You Don't Have

This seems like a relatively simple thing to do, but unfortunately product and purchase temptation exist. Whether it's a new iPhone, a car slightly above budget, or dining out with friends, you are tempted. The only thing you're thinking about is in the moment, but there are long-term consequences.

I constantly go over this with one of my daughters who has an addiction to using overdraft protection. The specific bank I will leave unnamed, but this added protection was something I found more hurtful than helpful to use especially with the overdraft fee being so large. No matter the amount she went over, be it a dollar or one hundred dollars, the fee was $36. Now this could be manageable if the cost wasn't $36 per transaction, and then on top of that, an extended overdraft fee of the same amount after a few days.

Occasionally, places will work with you on removing the overdraft charges, but you will rarely get more than one fee waived. If you choose to not pay it, the account will increase in debt until the account is charged off to a debt collector. Now this will show up on your credit report, lowering your credit score, and in turn, limiting you from important future loans, credit cards, and so much more.

- Simply save yourself the headache and save instead of spend.

Get a Job—Any Job:

- When you are working and have a routine and obligation, the way you view money changes.

- You can always work your way up if you remember to start.

- The value of money to you will increase when it's your money.

NOTES:

_____

_____

_____

_____

_____

_____

_____

_____

_____

_____

_____

_____

_____

_____

_____

Date:_____

NOTES:

_____

_____

_____

_____

_____

_____

_____

_____

_____

_____

_____

_____

_____

_____

Date:_____

NOTES:

Date:_____

"You don't make spending decisions, investment decisions, hiring decisions, or whether-you're-going-to-look-for-a-job decisions when you don't know what's going to happen."

—Michael Bloomberg

Chapter 2

Steady Cash Flow

After you get a job, it's very important to have a steady cash flow. The money coming in always needs to be more than your expenses and the money going out.

Maybe you counted your rent or mortgage, but don't forget to take into account gas in your car or other forms of transportation. Remember food, toiletries, and grooming services all are extra costs. Make sure your income covers it all.

Terms that you need to remember:

- Income: money earned or received from work or investments

- Net Worth: assets minus liabilities

- In your notes, document some ways you can get more income.

- Also note some unexpected expenses you had this week.

NOTES:

Date:

NOTES:

_____

_____

_____

_____

_____

_____

_____

_____

_____

_____

_____

_____

_____

_____

_____

_____

Date:_____

NOTES:

_____
_____
_____
_____
_____
_____
_____
_____
_____
_____
_____
_____
_____
_____
_____

Date:_____

"Too many people spend money they earned to buy things they don't want to impress people that they don't like."

—Will Rogers

Chapter 3

Cash, Not Credit

Appearances may be deceiving, especially with credit cards

Young college kids and unknowing adults are baited into getting credit cards with cash bonuses. Certain places offer gift cards or simply offer high limits. Banks encourage consumers to link credit cards to bank accounts as overdraft protection. Linking your card to your checking or savings account makes it easier for the credit card companies to take the money you owe them back. If you fall behind and/or miss a payment, it affects your credit score. The importance of your credit cannot be emphasized enough.

There are extenuating circumstances where getting a credit card is the better option over a loan or perhaps a late paycheck. However, this should not become a habit, as it can create a pattern of debt. One of my daughters decided to get a credit card with her bank. They gave her a limit of $2,000, and she spent every dollar. She figured with her job and refund check, she could pay it off. She did not take into account the interest.

What to watch out for:

- Interest
- Hidden Fees
- Signup Promises
- Terms and Conditions

NOTES:

_____

_____

_____

_____

_____

_____

_____

_____

_____

_____

_____

_____

_____

_____

_____

Date:_____

NOTES:

_____

_____

_____

_____

_____

_____

_____

_____

_____

_____

_____

_____

_____

_____

Date:_____

NOTES:

Date:_____

"You must gain control over your money, or the lack of it will forever control you.

—Dave Ramsey

Chapter

Turn Up Your Value

Learn. Read. Educate yourself.

I cannot emphasize this enough. You must continue to learn. Often, we get so caught up in grasping one thing that we get complacent.

Ways to learn

- Books
- Seminars
- Newspapers
- Online Articles

A few books you should read:

- *Rich Dad, Poor Dad*
- *The 48 Laws of Power*
- *The Wall Street Journal* (newspaper)

NOTES:

_____

_____

_____

_____

_____

_____

_____

_____

_____

_____

_____

_____

_____

Date:_____

NOTES:

___

Date:___

NOTES:

_____

_____

_____

_____

_____

_____

_____

_____

_____

_____

_____

_____

_____

_____

Date:_____

"Without continual growth and progress, such words as improvement, achievement, and success have no meaning."

—Benjamin Franklin

Chapter 5

Get Mentors

In life, it's sometimes hard to think beyond what we know, which is why we learn from others, whether it be a teacher in finance, a parent, or someone more publicly known for their achievements. Do not just pick someone who is successful. They must also be practical.

Notice your mentors' spending habits, practices, and investments. Note their mistakes and failures and how you can avoid them in the future.

If you have mentored your children at a young age, consider your time well invested. Please make sure your children have the tools to get to where they want to be and know how to use them.

Possible Mentors:

- Parents
- Teachers/Coaches
- Business Leaders
- Authors
- CEOs
- Someone who is what you want to be

NOTES:

_____

_____

_____

_____

_____

_____

_____

_____

_____

_____

_____

_____

_____

_____

_____

_____

Date:_____

NOTES:

_____
_____
_____
_____
_____
_____
_____
_____
_____
_____
_____
_____
_____

Date:_____

NOTES:

_____

_____

_____

_____

_____

_____

_____

_____

_____

_____

_____

_____

_____

_____

_____

Date:_____

Chapter 6

Avoid the Extra Pennies

The following all add up:

- The convenience fee of having your car delivered to you

- Money transfer fees from Western Union and Walmart

- Sending money from one bank to a different bank

- Getting gas from a higher-priced gas station

- Ride-sharing services such as Uber and Lyft

- TV subscription services such as Hulu and Netflix

Things that incur fees/additional costs:

- Loans
- Credit Cards
- Gas

NOTES:

Date:_____

NOTES:

_____

_____

_____

_____

_____

_____

_____

_____

_____

_____

_____

_____

_____

_____

_____

Date:_____

NOTES:

Date:_____

Chapter 7

Own Money

Often a lot of people limit the idea of money to government-printed bills or their current balance in their account. You need to have things of value that you can sell, auction, or lease. These things are not yet a form of tangible currency, but investing in them or having them in your possession is like owning money. It's always important to have assets you can liquidate. You can invest in or purchase things of value such as land, gold, diamonds, and bonds. Others might even go as far as to invest out of the country and later convert to have more than the US value.

Things worth money that can be consolidated:

- Gold
- Silver
- Pearls

- Bonds
- Stocks
- Houses

NOTES:

Date:_____

NOTES:

___

___

___

___

___

___

___

___

___

___

___

___

___

___

Date:_____

NOTES:

_____

_____

_____

_____

_____

_____

_____

_____

_____

_____

_____

_____

_____

_____

_____

Date:_____

"A successful man is one who can lay a firm foundation with the bricks others have thrown at him."

—David Brinkley

Chapter 8

A Membership Goes a Long Way

If you join a club, you get certain resources and perks. This saves you money in the long run. You receive better treatment and are more credible.

Things and places you can be a member of:

- Hotels
- AAA
- Entrepreneur organizations
- Speaker organization
- Timeshares
- Airlines

NOTES:

_____

_____

_____

_____

_____

_____

_____

_____

_____

_____

_____

_____

_____

Date:_____

NOTES:

_____

_____

_____

_____

_____

_____

_____

_____

_____

_____

_____

_____

_____

_____

_____

_____

Date:_____

NOTES:

_____
_____
_____
_____
_____
_____
_____
_____
_____
_____
_____
_____
_____
_____

Date:_____

"If you don't value your time, neither will others. Stop giving away your time and talents. Value what you know and start charging for it."

—Kim Garst

Chapter 9

Insure Yourself and Your Things

Better safe than sorry. Insure yourself and your things and have a plan.

Things to insure:

- Car
- House/Apartment
- Phone/Laptop/iPad
- Yourself
  - Will
  - Trust

Type of plans you need

- Dental
- Health
- Retirement (401k)
- Savings plan for children's education
- Payment plans

NOTES:

_____

_____

_____

_____

_____

_____

_____

_____

_____

_____

_____

_____

_____

_____

_____

_____

Date:_____

NOTES:

Date:_____

NOTES:

Date:_____

"Financial peace isn't the acquisition of stuff. It's learning to live on less than you make so you can give money back and have money to invest. You can't win until you do this."

—Dave Ramsey

My sincerest thanks to my daughter Adriana Gore, the publishers who made this book possible, my family, and my friends.

About the Author

Dr. Allen Gore is a psychiatrist living in Mitchellville, Maryland. He graduated from medical school at Drexel University in 1979 and received his MBA from the University of South Florida in 2000. He is a leading authority on rational behavioral therapy and served as Chief Resident and Fellow at the Rational Behavior Training Center in the Department of Psychiatry at the University of Kentucky College of Medicine.

Dr. Gore also has 46 years of experience studying and practicing martial arts. He was inducted into the Masters Hall of Fame in 2001, and into the USA International Black Belt Hall of Fame three years in a row from 2015 to 2017. Dr. Gore is married to minister Angelette Gore. He has six children (five daughters and one son) and a dog named Rocky. His hobbies include teaching and watching movies.

CREATING DISTINCTIVE BOOKS WITH INTENTIONAL RESULTS

We're a collaborative group of creative masterminds with a mission to produce high-quality books to position you for monumental success in the marketplace.

Our professional team of writers, editors, designers, and marketing strategists work closely together to ensure that every detail of your book is a clear representation of the message in your writing.

Want to know more?
Write to us at info@publishyourgift.com
or call (888) 949-6228

Discover great books, exclusive offers, and more at
www.PublishYourGift.com

Connect with us on social media

@publishyourgift

www.ingramcontent.com/pod-product-compliance
Lightning Source LLC
Chambersburg PA
CBHW071538080526
44588CB00011B/1722